For Yoona, and all the other young curious minds.
It's okay to fall. You can always get back up and try again.

ヴェラ・ウォン
Vera Wang

にぎやかなニューヨークに、ヴェラ・ウォンという女(おんな)の子(こ)がいました。ヴェラはスケートが大好(だいす)きで、まい日(にち)たくさんれんしゅうをしていました。きれいないしょうやおんがく、うつくしいうごきが大好(だいす)きで、いつかチャンピオンになることをゆめ見(み)ていました。

In bustling New York City, there was a little girl named Vera Wang. Vera enjoyed ice skating so much that she spent hours practicing almost every day. She loved the beautiful costumes, music, and graceful movements and dreamed of becoming a champion skater one day.

何年もいっしょうけんめいれんしゅうしたけれど、ヴェラはオリンピックのチームに入れませんでした。とてもかなしかったけれど、新しいことにちょうせんする時がきたと感じました。

But even though she worked really hard for years, Vera couldn't make it to the U.S. Olympic figure skating team. She felt sad but knew it was time to try different things and find other passions.

大学生になったヴェラは、フランスのパリで時間をすごすことにしました。パリでたくさんのきれいなものやスタイルに出会い、すぐにファッションにむちゅうになりました。

When Vera was in college, she decided to spend time in Paris, France, to explore a different part of the world. In Paris, she discovered many different styles and beautiful things. Soon, she fell in love with fashion!

それからヴェラは、有名なファッションざっしではたらくことにしました。ファッションについてまなびながら、新しいりゅうこうについて書いていました。たくさんの人が、そのざっしをたのしんでいました。

Naturally, Vera decided to work at a famous fashion magazine for her first job. She learned all about fashion and wrote stories about the latest trends. With her creativity and hard work, she published numerous magazines that millions of people enjoyed.

ヴェラはしごとが大好きでしたが、自分でようふくを作りたいと思うようになりました。大好きなしごとをやめるのはむずかしかったけれど、また新しいせかいにちょうせんする時がきたと感じていました。それで、大きなファッションの会社ではたらきはじめました。

Vera loved her job, but she aspired to create clothes, too. Although it wasn't easy to leave what she loved, she knew it was time to explore a new world, just as she had before. So, she joined a big fashion company.

でも、新しい会社では、会社のスタイルにあわせなければいけませんでした。ヴェラは、自分のアイデアをもっと自由にひょうげんしたいと思うようになりました。

However, Vera faced new challenges. Her imagination had to align with the company's style and direction. She craved the opportunity to fully express herself and bring her unique ideas to life.

ある日、ヴェラがけっこんする時、自分にぴったりのドレスをさがしていましたが、なかなか見つかりませんでした。

One day, when Vera was getting married, she searched for the perfect dress but couldn't find anything that felt right for her.

そこで、ヴェラは自分でドレスをデザインすることにきめました。そして、すぐに作りはじめました。

So she decided to design her own dress just the way she wanted. She put her plan into action right away.

ヴェラのドレスは、シンプルで、とても上品でした。
そして、自分にぴったりのドレスだとかんじました。

The dress was simple, elegant, and most importantly, it made her feel like herself.

みんながそのドレスをほめてくれたので、ヴェラはほかの人のためにもきれいなウェディングドレスを作りたいと思うようになりました。ちょっとこわかったけれど、ちょうせんするべきだとかんじました。

Everyone loved it so much that Vera thought she could make beautiful wedding gowns for others too. It was definitely a scary idea, but deep inside, she knew she should give it a try.

そこでヴェラは、ニューヨークに自分のお店をひらきました。ヴェラは、けっこんする人が、とくべつで、うつくしい気もちになれるようなドレスを作りたいと思っていました。

So Vera opened her own store in New York City. She wanted to create dresses that made every bride feel special and beautiful on their big day.

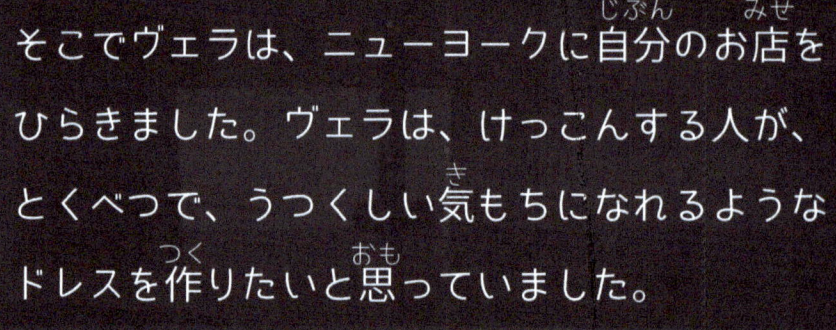

ヴェラのドレスはすぐに人気になり、有名な人たちもヴェラにドレスを作ってほしいとおねがいするようになりました。

Her unique designs quickly became so popular that many celebrities started asking her to make dresses for their weddings.

ヴェラのお店(みせ)がどんどん大(おお)きくなると、ヴェラは、たくさんのしょうをもらうようになりました。

As Vera's bridal shop grew, she received many awards for her stunning designs.

ヴェラのドレスは、ファッションざっしやテレビ、映画にも出るようになり、ヴェラはファッションのスターになりました。

Her dresses appeared in various fashion magazines, TV shows, and movies. Vera's talent and dedication made her a true fashion icon.

でも、ヴェラはそれだけで終わりませんでした。
もっと勇気を出して、メガネやこう水、ようふくや家の
かざりまで、作るようになりました。

But Vera didn't stop there. She took courage and expanded her brand to include eyewear, perfumes, ready-to-wear collections, and even home décor.

小さなお店だったのに、今ではせかい中で愛される大きなブランドになりました。

Her small shop grew into a massive, international brand that many people around the world loved.

ヴェラにとって、ファッションは
スケートとよくにていました。
スピードやいきおいがあります。

For Vera, fashion was very similar to skating. There's speed, and there's movement.

ころんでも、また 立ち上がって、
ちょうせんするひつようがあります。

When you fall, you need to get up and try again.

だんだんと、ヴェラは、そんなちょうせんを、たのしめるようになっていきました。

Over time, she learned to embrace and move through these challenges with joy.

ヴェラは、こわがってもだいじょうぶだと
おしえてくれました。大切なのは、まえを
むいて、勇気をもって、新しいことに
ちょうせんすることです。

Vera taught us that it's okay to be scared.
The important thing is to look forward,
be brave, and try new things.

もし、とびらがしまってしまっても、
また立ち上がって、べつのとびらを
さがせばいいのです。

If some doors are closed, you can always
get up and look for another door!

The Story of Vera Wang

Little Vera, the Skater

Vera Dreaming of Joining the Olympic Team

Vera's Wedding Day

Vera Wang's journey in fashion didn't happen overnight—it was built on years of hard work and a willingness to try new things. After the disappointment of not making the Olympic skating team, Vera could have given up on her dreams. Instead, she sought out new passions, and that decision changed her life.

When her first bridal designs were praised, Vera didn't stop there. She knew success wouldn't come easily, so she continued to push boundaries,

Vera's First Bridal Shop in 1990

Vera's Beautiful Dress on a TV Show

Receiving the National Medal of the Arts

expanding her work into new fields like evening gowns, perfumes, and even home décor.

Her resilience paid off, and she became one of the most famous designers in the world, known not only for her stunning creations but also for her spirit of constant growth and learning. Vera Wang's story shows that when life takes an unexpected turn, staying strong and believing in yourself can lead to extraordinary achievements.

© Copyright 2024 - Yeonsil Yoo, all rights reserved.
Paperback ISBN: 978-1-998277-51-3
Hardback ISBN: 978-1-998277-52-0

www.upflybooks.com

No part of this publication may be reproduced, stored in a retrieval system, or transmitted in any form or by any means, electronic, mechanical, photocopying, recording, or otherwise, without the prior written permission of the publisher, except as permitted under copyright law.

Photographic acknowledgments (pages 30-31):
Vera Wang's Instagram and X (@VeraWang)
Penske Media via Getty Images for Vera Wang's First Bridal Shop
Photo by Patrick Demarchelier, Vogue, June 2008, featuring Sarah Jessica Parker

Other Bilingual Japanese-English Books by the Author

Get Your Next eBook for FREE! Scan the QR code or visit upflybooks.com to sign up as a beta reader!

www.ingramcontent.com/pod-product-compliance
Lightning Source LLC
Chambersburg PA
CBHW061351010526
44107CB00011B/900